MEDIC MARVELS

Inspiring True Stories of the Scientists who Changed Medicine

Oussama Wail BOUHENTALA

M.D Epidemiologist

Preface:

Have you ever wondered how we went from battling the bubonic plague to video games in just a few hundred years?!! The truth is, our comfortable lives today are thanks to a whole team of **real-life superheroes**! Forget capes and tights, these heroes wielded scalpels, microscopes, and an unshakeable determination to make the world a healthier place.

This book isn't your typical history lesson. We'll journey through time to meet these incredible men and women, the doctors, nurses, and scientists who fought tirelessly against disease. But instead of dusty textbooks, we'll use a touch of humor (think silly jokes, not gross medical stuff!) to make their stories exciting and relatable, especially for young readers.

Why superheroes, you ask? Because facing down deadly illnesses deserves a medal, don't you think? These heroes dedicated their lives to saving others, and their superpowers? Determination, perseverance, and a whole lot of love for science and humanity.

This book isn't just about exciting tales, though. It's about paying tribute to these real-life heroes and inspiring the next generation of future doctors, nurses, and maybe even a few future scientists! So, buckle up, grab your magnifying glass (optional, but cool!), and get ready to meet the **Medic MARVELS** who made our world a healthier place!

Table of Content

1. The Germ Buster: how Edward Jenner saved the world……………………………………………………………………5
2. Clean Hands, Healthy Lives: The Tale of Dr. Ignaz ….. 8
3. Battling the Breath Thief: Koch, Calmette & Guérin and the BCG Vaccine ………………………………………… 13
4. Paving the Way, Elizabeth Blackwell: America's First Woman Doctor…………………………………………………… 17
5. Dr. William and the Magic Sleep Gas. ………………… 20
6. Wilhelm and the secret rays. …………………………… 23
7. Doctor Alphonse and the Mysterious Mosquitoes . 27
8. Battling the Breath Thief: Louis Pasteur and Germs 31
9. Polio Busters: Salk vs. Sabin - The Vaccine Showdown! ………………………………………………………… 34
10. Moldy Mess Saves the Day: The Story of Alexander Fleming and Penicillin …………………………………………. 38
11. The Glowy Gunk Chronicles : Marie Curie, the Radioactive Rock Star! ……………………………………… 42
12. The OG Doc: Al-Zahrawi, the Medieval Medical Mastermind………………………………………………………. 45
13. Sugar Sleuth: Gerty Cori and the Mystery of Muscle Power……………………………………………………………… 48
14. Doc Dread vs. the Deadly Downpour: How John Snow Stopped a Poop Problem ………………………… 52
15. Battlefield Babe Saves the Day: Florence Nightingale, the Nurse with the Glowing Up! ………………………… 56

16. Banting & Best, the Diabetic Dudes! 61
17. The OG Doc Rock Star: Avicenna, the Prince of Physicians! 65
18. Stetho-Spy: René Laënnec's Heartbeat Heroics! 70
19. The Heart Hacker: Christiaan Barnard, the Doc Who Swapped Beating Boxes! 74
20. The Smell Superstar: Dr. Linda B. Buck, the Queen of Funky Funky Smells! 79
21. The OG Spare Parts Doc: Dr. Joseph Murray, the Kidney Kick-Starter! 83
22. Dr. Crumpler: First Black Woman Doctor (Seriously!) 87
23. The Dude Who Saved Lives with... Stinky Spray? ... 90
24. The Body Dude: Andreas Vesalius and the Exploding Skeleton 92
25. About the Author 100

The Germ Buster: how Edward Jenner saved the world.

Have you ever heard of smallpox? It was a super scary disease that made people really sick, covered them in bumps, and could even kill them! Back in the 1700s, when my grand grandpa was a kid, it was everywhere. But then this cool dude named **Edward Jenner** came along and changed everything.

Jenner wasn't your typical doctor in a big fancy city hospital. He lived in a cozy village in England and treated everyone from farmers with sore throats to cows with moo-ffles (that's a cow cough, in case you didn't know). One thing he noticed was that milkmaids who got a mild illness called cowpox never seemed to catch the awful smallpox. It was like having cowpox made them invincible to the bigger germ bully!

This got Jenner thinking. What if he could use cowpox to protect people from smallpox? It sounded crazy, but Jenner was a brave scientist. In 1796, he took a tiny bit of pus (gross, I know, but that's what they used back then) from a milkmaid's cowpox blister and scratched it into the arm of a young boy named James Phipps. Imagine letting a doctor give you a scratch with something icky from a cow!

A few days later, James felt a little under the weather, but that was it. Then, Jenner tried exposing James to real smallpox, the super scary kind. And guess what? James didn't get sick! It worked! Jenner had invented the world's first vaccine, a way to train your body to fight a disease without getting really sick.

People didn't believe him at first. They thought he was messing around with cow germs. But slowly, more and more people got vaccinated, and fewer and fewer got smallpox. It was like a shield against a monster!
Thanks to Edward Jenner, the world became a much healthier place. Smallpox is almost gone now, and all because a curious country doctor wasn't afraid to try something new. So next time you get a vaccine, remember Edward Jenner, the germ buster who showed us the power of a tiny scratch and a big idea!

Edward Jenner
"The Father of Immunology"

1749 – 1823
England

Clean Hands, Healthy Lives: The Tale of Dr. Ignaz

Have you ever heard of "Mommy Fever"? It wasn't a real fever you could catch from your mom's hugs (although those can be pretty powerful). Back in the 1800s, lots of moms got very sick after having babies. This scary sickness was called puerperal fever, and it was a real bummer.

Imagine a doctor named **Ignaz Semmelweis**. He wasn't just any doctor, he worked in a special hospital room for new moms and their babies. But something terrible was happening. In Dr. Semmelweis' room, way too many moms were getting sick with Mommy Fever, and some even died! It was like a mystery illness.

The other doctors were confused. They tried everything – special diets, fancy medicines, even lucky charms (probably not that helpful). But nothing worked. Dr. Semmelweis was super worried. He just had to figure out what was making the moms sick.

Here's the weird part: in another room at the same hospital, there were way fewer sick moms. What was different? Dr. Semmelweis became a super sleuth. He compared everything – the rooms, the doctors, the moms' snacks (probably not that important). Finally, he noticed a big difference: the doctors in the room with fewer sick moms did something different after examining dead bodies. They washed their hands with a special chlorine solution! Aha! Dr. Semmelweis had a hunch. Maybe something invisible was getting on the doctors' hands from the dead bodies, and then they were spreading it to the moms! It sounded crazy, but he decided to try something. He made all the doctors in his room wash their hands with the chlorine solution before seeing any moms.

And guess what? The number of sick moms dropped dramatically! Dr. Semmelweis had solved the mystery! It wasn't ghosts or curses, it was invisible germs that could be washed away with soap and water. Talk about a superhero power!

Even though Dr. Semmelweis' idea was simple, some other doctors didn't believe him at first. But slowly, more and more hospitals started washing hands, and Mommy Fever became much less common. Dr. Semmelweis showed us that something as small as a good handwashing can be a giant germ fighter!

Ignaz Semmelweis

1818 - 1865

Hungary

EVERYDAY HYGIENE
6 Steps to Thorough Hand Washing
DON'T SKIP ANY STEP!

1. Wet
WET YOUR HANDS WITH CLEAN WATER.

2. Lather
LATHER YOUR HANDS BY RUBBING IT WITH SOAP.

3. Scrub
SCRUB YOUR HANDS, IN BETWEEN YOUR FINGERS, AND UNDER YOUR NAILS FOR AT LEAST 20 SECONDS.

4. Rinse
RINSE YOUR HANDS UNDER CLEAN RUNNING WATER.

5. Dry
DRY YOUR HANDS USING A CLEAN TOWEL OR TISSUE. YOU CAN ALSO AIR-DRY THEM.

6. Repeat
WASH YOUR HANDS AS OFTEN AS NECESSARY, ESPECIALLY BEFORE AND AFTER HANDLING FOOD.

DID YOU KNOW?

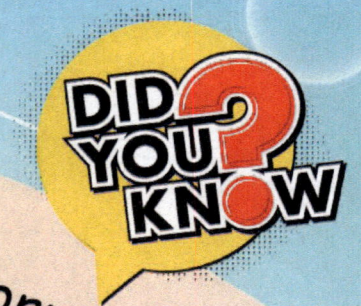

Babies are born with 300 bones, but as they grow, some bones fuse together, leaving adults with 206 bones.

Battling the Breath Thief: Koch, Calmette & Guérin and the BCG Vaccine

Imagine a monster that steals your breath, leaving you weak and coughing. That was tuberculosis (TB) back in the day. It was a terrible disease that could take your loved ones away. But three scientists – **Robert Koch, Albert Calmette, and Camille Guérin** – decided to fight back!

Robert Koch, the Germ Hunter from Germany (Clausthal, December 11, 1843): First came Dr. Koch, a superstar scientist from Germany who loved hunting down the tiniest troublemakers – germs! In 1882, he did something amazing: he identified the germ that caused TB! This was a huge breakthrough, like finding the villain's hideout! But just knowing the enemy wasn't enough. They needed a weapon. He was awarded the **Nobel Prize in Medicine in 1905** for his groundbreaking work on tuberculosis and infectious diseases.

Enter Calmette and Guérin, the French Vaccine Dream Team (Nice, France, July 12, 1863 for Calmette . Camille Guérin, birthdate unknown): Across the English Channel in France, Dr. Albert Calmette and Dr. Camille Guérin joined forces. They were like a superhero duo, determined to create a shield against TB. Their idea? Use a weakened version of the TB germ itself to train the body to fight it off!

Operation: Weaken the Wumpus: It wasn't easy. Imagine trying to turn a grumpy monster into a cuddly teddy bear. That's what Calmette and Guérin were trying to do with the TB germ. For years, they experimented, carefully weakening the germ over hundreds of generations. It was like training a tiny wrestler to become a gentle tickle fighter.

Albert Calmette (1863-1933)

Camille Guérin (1872-1961)

The BCG is Born!: Finally, in 1921, after almost 15 years of work, they had a champion – the Bacille Calmette-Guérin, or BCG vaccine! This weakened germ could be safely given to people, teaching their bodies to recognize and fight off the real TB monster. It was like giving everyone a tiny practice fight against the villain!

A Breath of Fresh Air: The BCG vaccine wasn't perfect, but it was a game-changer. It helped protect millions from the horrors of TB. Today, thanks to Koch, Calmette, and Guérin, TB is much less scary. We can all breathe a little easier because of their amazing work! While Calmette and Guérin didn't receive a Nobel Prize for their work on the BCG vaccine, their contribution to public health has saved countless lives.

Robert Koch
1843 – 1910
Noble Prize in Medicine 1905
Germany

Paving the Way, Elizabeth Blackwell: America's First Woman Doctor.

Imagine a time when girls weren't allowed to be doctors, no matter how smart or determined they were. That's the world Elizabeth Blackwell stepped into in 1821. Born in Bristol, England (February 3, 1821), she and her family moved to the United States when she was young. Elizabeth saw firsthand how many women suffered without proper medical care. Unlike most girls back then, Elizabeth's parents believed in education for all. This fueled her dream of becoming a doctor, a path completely closed to women at the time. But Elizabeth wouldn't be discouraged. She persisted, studying tirelessly and even teaching for a while to earn money for medical school.

Facing Rejection: Getting into medical school was a battle in itself. Every school Elizabeth applied to rejected her simply because she was a woman. Undeterred, she finally secured a spot at Geneva Medical College in New York in 1847. The all-male student body wasn't exactly welcoming, but Elizabeth persevered.

Breaking Barriers: In 1849, Elizabeth became the first woman in the United States to graduate from medical school. It was a huge victory, but the fight wasn't over. Hospitals wouldn't hire her, so she opened her own clinic in New York City in 1851. It catered to women and children, who often felt uncomfortable with male doctors.

A Legacy of Change: Elizabeth's success paved the way for other women in medicine. In 1857, she co-founded *the New York Infirmary for Women and Children*, the first hospital in the US staffed by women doctors. She also championed education for women doctors, opening a medical college for women at the infirmary in 1868. Elizabeth Blackwell's courage and determination broke down barriers for generations of women who followed her dream of becoming a doctor. Today, women make up a significant portion of the medical field, and that's all thanks to pioneers like Elizabeth Blackwell!.

Elizabeth Blackwell

1821 - 1910

United Kingdom

DID YOU KNOW?

Crybaby Alert!!!

Did you know that grown adults are basically giant walking water balloons? We're made up of about 60% water, but babies are even more hydrated – they're closer to 80% water! That's why they cry so much – they're basically leaking!

Dr. William and the Magic Sleep Gas.

Imagine a world where surgery meant gritting your teeth and bearing the pain. That was the reality until a dentist named **William Thomas Green Morton** came along. Born on August 9, 1819, in Charlton, Massachusetts, Morton witnessed the suffering his patients endured during dental procedures. He knew there had to be a better way.

Early Strides: Morton didn't start his career in medicine. He worked as a clerk, printer, and salesman before enrolling in dental school in Baltimore in 1840. After graduating, he practiced dentistry in Boston, where he witnessed firsthand the limitations of pain management.

A Spark of Inspiration:

In 1844, Morton attended a lecture where a dentist named Horace Wells demonstrated the use of nitrous oxide, also known as laughing gas, to reduce pain during dental procedures. While the demonstration wasn't entirely successful, it planted a seed in Morton's mind. He became obsessed with finding a safe and reliable way to numb pain during surgery.

Experimentation:

Morton experimented with various substances, including ether, a common solvent used at the time. After witnessing its anesthetic effects during a dental procedure in 1844, he began testing ether on animals. Finally, on October 16, 1846, at the Massachusetts General Hospital, Morton successfully used ether anesthesia during surgery for the first time.

Revolution in Medicine:

The news of Morton's discovery spread like wildfire. While the credit for anesthesia is debated Morton's public demonstration marked a turning point in medicine. Surgery could now be performed with significantly less pain for the patient.

Life After Ether:

Morton spent the rest of his life advocating for the use of anesthesia and battling legal disputes over patent rights. Though his later years were marked by financial difficulties, his contribution to medicine remains undeniable.

A Legacy of Comfort:

Thanks to Dr. William Morton's pioneering spirit, patients today

have access to various safe and effective anesthesia options, making surgery a less traumatic experience.

Wilhelm and the secret rays.

Imagine a time when doctors couldn't see inside your body without cutting you open. That's how it was before a smart scientist named **Wilhelm Conrad Röntgen** made an amazing discovery. He was born on March 27, 1845, in Germany and loved exploring the invisible world around us.

When he was young, his family moved to the Netherlands. Röntgen was really good at science and math, and he went to a special school in Switzerland. There, he learned a lot from famous scientists who encouraged his curiosity.

In 1895, while working in his lab in Germany, Röntgen noticed something weird. He was working with invisible rays called **cathode rays**, and even though he covered his machine with black paper, a nearby screen started to glow. Curious, Röntgen spent weeks studying this strange glow, realizing that these rays could pass through solid objects!

Röntgen called these mysterious rays "X-rays" because he didn't know exactly what they were. He took a picture of his wife's hand, showing her bones and her wedding ring. This discovery was huge because it allowed doctors to see inside the human body without cutting it open.

In 1901, Röntgen was awarded **the very first Nobel Prize in Physics** for discovering X-rays. He decided not to make money from his discovery so that it could help as many people as possible.

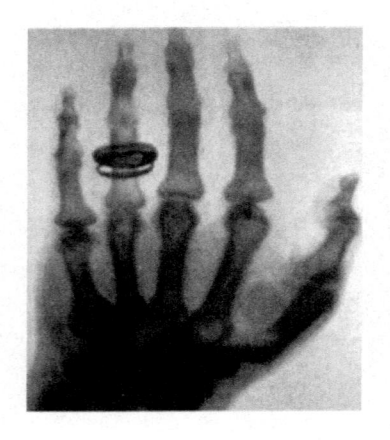

Today, X-rays are very important in medicine. They help doctors find broken bones and other illnesses. Thanks to Wilhelm Conrad Röntgen, we can see inside our bodies without any cuts, making medical treatments much easier and safer.

Wilhelm Conrad Röntgen
1845 – 1923.

the first Noble Prize for physics in 1901

Germany

HEALTHY SNACKS
FOR YOUR KIDS

FRUIT SMOOTHIE

COTTAGE CHEESE

YOGURT

HARD-BOILED EEG

BAKED SWEET POTATO FRIES

PEANUT

OATMEAL

Doctor Alphonse and the Mysterious Mosquitoes

Imagine a time when nobody knew what caused malaria, a serious and often deadly disease. That was the world before a determined French doctor named **Alphonse Laveran** made an important discovery. Born in Paris on June 18, 1845, Laveran loved medicine from a young age.

Early Life and Medical Career

Laveran went to medical school in Strasbourg, France. He became a military surgeon during the Franco-Prussian War. After the war, he kept working in medicine and joined the French army's medical service in **Algeria** (a beautiful country located in north Africa 😊) in 1878.

Solving the Malaria Mystery

In Algeria, malaria was a big problem for soldiers and local people. Laveran was very interested in figuring out what caused the disease. He carefully studied blood samples from people with malaria.

A Major Discovery

In 1880, Laveran found tiny parasites, now called **Plasmodium**, inside the red blood cells of malaria patients. This was a huge breakthrough because people used to think malaria was caused by bad air, not by parasites.

More Research and Recognition

Laveran kept studying the malaria parasite and its life cycle. His research helped develop new treatments and ways to prevent the disease. In 1907, he won the Nobel Prize in Medicine for his important discovery.

Fighting Malaria

Laveran's work helped create effective medicines and prevention methods that greatly reduced malaria around the world. Today, scientists still build on his research to fight malaria.

Other Contributions

Besides his malaria work, Laveran also studied other parasitic diseases like trypanosomiasis. He started the Laboratory of Tropical Medicine at the Pasteur Institute in Paris, contributing to the fields of parasitology and tropical medicine.

A Medical Pioneer

Alphonse Laveran's dedication to understanding malaria changed how we fight this terrible disease. His discovery shows how powerful scientific research can be in improving our health..

MAKE ME Smile

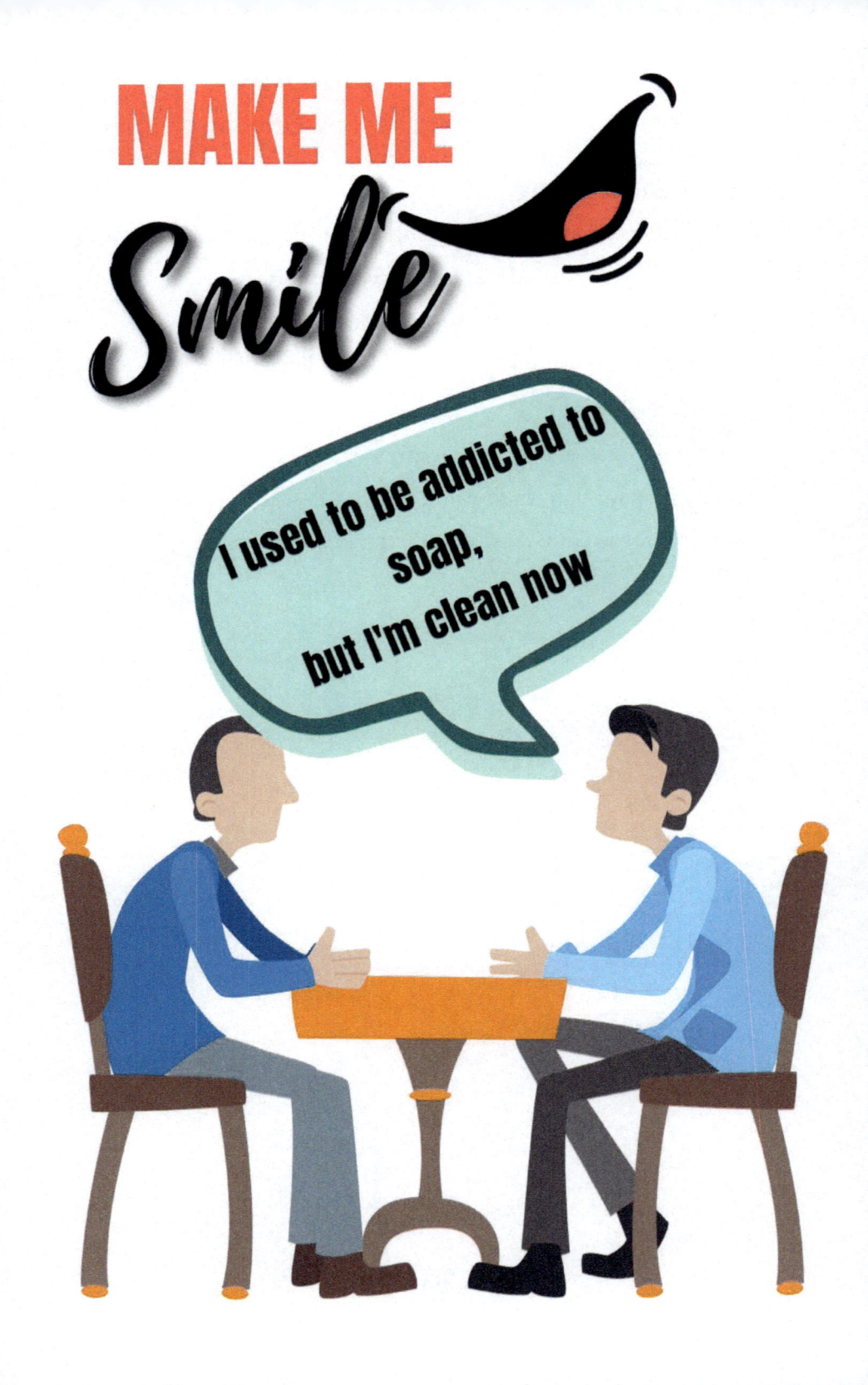

"I used to be addicted to soap, but I'm clean now"

Battling the Breath Thief: Louis Pasteur and Germs

Imagine a time when people got sick and nobody knew why or how to make them better. That's when Louis Pasteur, a super smart scientist, came in and changed everything. He was born on December 27, 1822, in Dole, France. Pasteur's curiosity led to discoveries that changed our understanding of dise.

Early Life and Studies

Pasteur started by studying crystals, but soon he got interested in how things like bread rise and wine ferments. He found out that tiny living things called microorganisms, like yeast, were responsible for fermentation. People used to think it happened by chance, but he proved them wrong.

Discovering Germs

This made Pasteur wonder if these tiny microorganisms could

cause diseases too. In the 1860s, he studied sick silkworms and chickens and showed that specific germs caused their illnesses. This idea, called the germ theory of disease, was a big deal because people believed that bad air caused diseases.

Helping Industries and Saving Lives

Pasteur's work wasn't just for science books. He found ways to stop mile and beer from spoiling by killing harmful bacteria. This process is called pasteurization. It saved the milk and wine industries and made food safer for everyone.

Inventing Vaccines

Pasteur also invented vaccines, which are weakened germs that help our bodies learn to fight diseases. His most famous success was **the rabies vaccine**, which saved many lives. He also made a vaccine for chicken cholera, proving that vaccines could stop diseases.

A Lasting Impact

Pasteur's work changed medicine forever. The germ theory led to better hygiene practices and the development of antibiotics. His vaccines continue to save millions of lives from diseases like rabies, polio, and measles.

Beyond Science

Pasteur did more than just make discoveries. He showed the

importance of careful experiments and challenged old ideas. His dedication to science and health still inspires researchers today.

Louis Pasteur: More Than Pasteurization

Pasteurization is one of his famous contributions, but Pasteur's impact on science and medicine is much bigger. He was a true scientific hero, whose work helps us fight diseases and stay healthy even now.

Louis Pasteur
1822 - 1895
France

Polio Busters: Salk vs. Sabin - The Vaccine Showdown!

Imagine summer vacation, but you can't go to the pool because of a scary disease called polio. It could mess you up bad, leaving you all wobbly and weak. Two super scientists, ***Jonas Salk &Albert Sabin***, were like superheroes in this battle!

Salk: The Injectable Ironman

This American dude, Salk, born in 1914 (way before smartphones!), believed in a super-soldier approach. His vaccine used dead polio germs, like showing your body mugshots of the bad guys, so it could recognize and fight them off if they ever showed up for real. In 1952, after tons of experiments, Salk's injectable vaccine was a total win!

National Hero Alert!

By 1955, Salk's vaccine was everywhere, making him a mega-star! Kids were lining up for shots, and polio cases started dropping like flies. This was awesome, but there was a catch. You needed a few shots, and it didn't protect against all the different types of polio germs.

Enter Sabin: The Sweet Solution

Meanwhile, another scientist named Albert Sabin, born in Poland in 1906 (also way before video games!), had a different plan. His vaccine used weakened, LIVE polio germs, but don't worry, they were too wimpy to make you sick! These guys would train your body's defenses even better, and it only needed drops on a sugar cube – way cooler than a shot!

The Oral Polio Smackdown!

Sabin's vaccine came out in the late 1950s. It was easier to give, especially in faraway places, and protected against more polio types. By the 1960s, this sweet solution became the go-to vaccine in many countries.

Teamwork Makes the Dream Work!

Even though Salk and Sabin had different ideas, they both wanted the same thing: to CRUSH polio! Salk's vaccine was the first punch, and Sabin's vaccine kept polio down for the count. Today, thanks to them, polio is almost GONE! That's what happens when super scientists work together, even if there's a little friendly competition!

DID YOU KNOW?

The fastest muscle in your body is the blink reflex. It can close your eyelid in a mere 1/3 of a second, protecting your eye from danger.

Moldy Mess Saves the Day: The Story of Alexander Fleming and Penicillin

Imagine you're playing video games, totally zoned in, when BAM! You get hit with a super nasty infection. Back in the day, before awesome antibiotics, these infections could really wreck your game. But then a dude named **Alexander Fleming** stepped in, and things got interesting, thanks to some moldy mess!

Fleming: The Messy Genius

Born in Scotland in 1881 (way before computers!), Fleming wasn't the neatest guy. But hey, being messy can lead to cool discoveries, right? Fleming loved studying germs, those tiny villains that make you sick. One day, after forgetting to clean up his petri dish (think science experiment plate), he noticed something weird – mold growing on it! Gross, right? But here's the kicker: wherever the mold was, the nasty germs were GONE!

Penicillin: The Weapon from Mold

Fleming figured this mold was making a special weapon against the germs. He named it penicillin, after the mold (Penicillium not-atum, that's the sciencey name). The problem? Getting enough of this penicillin to actually fight infections. It took years of work by other scientists (like teammates in a game!) to make it a usable medicine.

From Mess to Medicine!

Finally, in the 1940s, penicillin became a game-changer! Soldiers in World War II were getting saved from deadly infections, and people everywhere were getting healthy again. Fleming, the messy genius, became a total rockstar!

Fleming's Legacy: Beyond the Mold

Even though penicillin wasn't perfect (some germs learned to dodge it!), it opened the door for a whole bunch of other antibiotics. Today, thanks to Fleming's moldy discovery, we have tons of weapons to fight infections and keep ourselves healthy. So next time you take an antibiotic, remember the messy genius and his moldy friend who started it all!

"One sometimes finds what one is not looking for " , Fleming ,Alxendre

Alexander Fleming
1881 – 1955
Nobel Prize in Medicine 1945

United Kingdom

The Glowy Gunk Chronicles : Marie Curie, the Radioactive Rock Star!

Imagine a world with NO X-ray machines for broken bones! Yuck! That's how it was before this super cool scientist named Marie Curie came along. Born Marie Sklodowska in 1867 (way before smartphones!), she was a total rock star in the science world, especially for girls, because science wasn't really for them back then. That didn't stop Marie!

Marie and the Mystery Goo
Marie hung out in Paris with her scientist husband Pierre, and they both loved messing around with glowy rocks. One day, Marie noticed this weird, glowing gunk that made things zap like a weak taser. They called it radioactivity, because its rays were like invisible punches. But here's the coolest part: this gunk could also see through stuff! Imagine seeing your friend's

hidden candy stash with X-ray vision – epic!

Double-Nobel-Winning Ninja

In 1903, Marie and Pierre, along with another scientist buddy, won a Nobel Prize, which is like a super-science award, for finding radioactivity. But wait, there's more! After Pierre sadly passed away, Marie kept going and won another Nobel Prize in 1911, all by herself! This girl was unstoppable!

Glowing Legacy: From Rocks to Rad Treatments
Marie's radioactive rocks ended up being super useful for doctors. X-rays helped them see broken bones, and scientists figured out ways to use radiation to fight yucky diseases too. Even though too much radiation is bad (like eating too much candy!), Marie's discovery changed medicine forever.

So next time you get an X-ray, or hear about radiation treatments, remember Marie Curie, the girl who wasn't afraid of glowy rocks and changed the world!

Marie Curie
1867 – 1934
Noble prize in Physics 1903
Noble prize in Chemistry 1911

Poland

The OG Doc: Al-Zahrawi, the Medieval Medical Mastermind

Imagine a time before fancy hospitals and video game surgery simulations. That was the world Al-Zahrawi lived in, way back in 10th century **Andalusia** (that's modern-day Spain and Portugal). But even without all the high-tech stuff, Al-Zahrawi became a mega-doc legend!

From Butcher to Bandage Boss

Born around 940 AD (that's way before even sliced bread!), Al-Zahrawi wasn't always a medical mastermind. He started as a barber-surgeon, which basically meant he cut hair and, well, did some surgery too (yikes!). But Al-Zahrawi wasn't a fan of chopping people up blindly. He craved knowledge and spent years studying old medical texts and even dissecting bodies (ew, but super important for learning!).

The Book of Cool Surgery Tricks

After all that studying, Al-Zahrawi wrote a medical encyclopedia called "The Book of Guiding Knowledge." This book was EPIC! It had tons of amazing surgical techniques, including cool stuff like using catgut (made from cat intestines, TMI?) for stitches and even inventing new tools for operating. Doctors everywhere were like "Whoa, this Al-Zahrawi dude is on to something!"

Beyond the Battlefield

Al-Zahrawi wasn't just a whiz with scalpels. He also wrote about how to take care of injuries, set broken bones, and even treat eye problems. Back then, war was pretty common, so Al-Zahrawi's skills were lifesaving for soldiers on the battlefield.

A Legacy that Healed the World

Al-Zahrawi's book became a mega-hit in the medical

world, translated into different languages and used by doctors for centuries! His ideas even influenced surgery in Europe. So next time you get a bandage or stitches, remember Al-Zahrawi, the OG doc who paved the way for modern medicine with his guts (literally, with the catgut stitches) and genius!

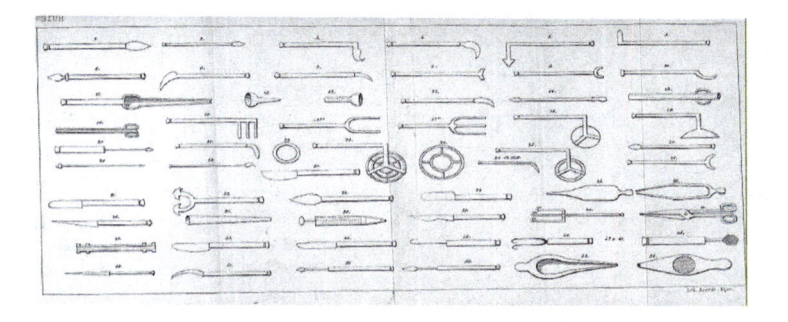

Surgical instruments Abulcasis 1861.
Source : http://web2.bium.univ-paris5.fr/livanc/?cote=30707&p=363&do=page « book scan ».
Author : Dr Lucien Leclerc

Sugar Sleuth: Gerty Cori and the Mystery of Muscle Power

Imagine you're running a marathon, pushing your limits. But your muscles feel sluggish, like they're running out of fuel. That's where **Gerty Cori** comes in, a brilliant biochemist who cracked the code of how our bodies use sugar for energy!

From Curious Kid to Chemistry Champ

Born Gerty Radnitz in 1896 (way before energy drinks!), Gerty was a curious kid in Prague who loved figuring things out. Even though girls weren't really encouraged to study science back then, Gerty didn't care. She aced her classes and eventually went to medical school, where she met her future partner-in-science, Carl Cori.

Teaming Up with Mr. Cori

Gerty and Carl were a super-science duo. They both loved figuring out the mysteries of the human body, especially how we use energy. They focused on a type of sugar called glucose, the fuel that keeps our muscles moving. But where did this sugar come from, and where did it go after we used it?

The Cori Cycle: Sugar's Secret Journey

Gerty and Carl spent years experimenting, and guess what? They cracked the code! They discovered a cycle, now called the Cori Cycle, that explains how sugar travels through our bodies. Muscles store sugar called glycogen, and when we need a burst of energy, the Cori Cycle kicks in, turning glycogen back into glucose to power our muscles. Then, when we're resting, the cycle reverses, storing extra glucose back as glycogen. Pretty cool, right?

Double Nobel Glory!

In 1947, Gerty and Carl, along with another scientist, were awarded the Nobel Prize for their amazing discovery. Gerty was only the third woman EVER to win a science Nobel Prize – a huge win for girls in science everywhere!

Gerty's Legacy: A Sweeter Future for Health

Understanding how our bodies use sugar is super important. Gerty's work helps scientists develop treatments for diabetes and other diseases related to energy metabolism. So next time you grab a snack for a quick energy boost, remember Gerty Cori, the sugar sleuth who unlocked the secrets of muscle power!

DID YOU KNOW?

There are more bacteria in your mouth than there are people on Earth! Thankfully, most of them are harmless.

Doc Dread vs. the Deadly Downpour: How John Snow Stopped a Poop Problem

Imagine a summer vacation ruined by a nasty stomach bug. Yuck! Well, in the 1800s in London, things were way worse. A super-icky illness called cholera was spreading like wildfire, causing terrible diarrhea and leaving people dehydrated and weak. That's where **Dr. John Snow** comes in, a detective doc determined to stop this smelly situation!

Doc Dread on the Case

Born in 1799 (way before indoor plumbing!), John Snow wasn't your average doctor. He wasn't afraid to get his hands dirty investigating diseases. When the cholera outbreak hit London, finger-pointing flew everywhere.

People blamed "bad air," but Doc Snow wasn't buying it. He knew something else was going on.

The Poop Pointing Puzzle

Snow started mapping out where cholera cases were popping up. He noticed a cluster around a specific public water pump on Broad Street. Eww, gross! But Snow suspected something – maybe the water was making people sick!

The Pump Problem

Snow convinced officials to shut down the Broad Street pump. Guess what? Cholera cases around that pump PLUMMETED! It turned out sewage from leaky toilets was seeping into the water supply, making people sick. Doc Dread had cracked the case!

A Hero for Health

Snow's detective work changed the game. People started paying attention to clean water and sanitation. His ideas helped prevent future cholera outbreaks and saved countless lives.

Doc Snow's Legacy: Beyond the Poop Problem

Even though Snow couldn't see the tiny germs causing cholera, his work laid the foundation for the science of **epidemiology**, which is like disease detective work 😊 Today, thanks to Doc Snow, we have cleaner water systems and a better understanding of how diseases spread.

So next time you take a clean sip of water, remember Dr. John Snow, the detective doc who wasn't afraid to get to the bottom of a smelly situation and stopped a poop problem from becoming a citywide disaster!

This water's giving everyone the grumbles!
Hey, blame the pipes, not me!

Battlefield Babe Saves the Day: Florence Nightingale, the Nurse with the Glowing Up!

Imagine a war zone like a video game, but way worse – no respawn points, and if you got hurt, you might actually die from like, dirty bandages. That's what things were like for soldiers in the 1800s. Then ***Florence Nightingale*** shows up, a total badass nurse who wasn't afraid of anything, not even creepy crawlies in the hospital (eww!).

From Prissy Princess to Powerful Nurse

Born in 1820 (long before video games!), Florence wasn't your typical girly-girl. She ditched fancy dresses to take care of sick people, which wasn't exactly cool for girls back then. But Florence didn't care. She followed her heart and trained to be a nurse in Germany – that's like super far away back then, with no airplanes!

The Crimean Catastrophe – No Time for Video Games!

There was a big war going on called the Crimean War, and the hospitals for the soldiers were a total disaster zone – dark, dirty, and more crowded than a school cafeteria at lunch. When Florence heard about it, she was like, "Hold my bandages!" She gathered a crew of nurses and headed straight for the battlefield.

Shining Bright Like a Diamond (Well, Almost)

What Florence saw was nightmare-ish: smelly rooms, grumpy soldiers with infected wounds, and way too many people dying. But Florence wasn't scared. She cleaned everything up, kicked out the creepy crawlies (eww again!), and even held soldiers' hands and cheered them up. She even carried a lamp on her night rounds, which is why they called her "The Lady with the Lamp" – way cooler than any superhero name!

Nightingale's Legacy: More Than Just Bandages

Florence didn't just help soldiers during the war. She totally changed nursing forever! She made sure nurses had proper training, hospitals were clean, and most importantly, that patients were treated with kindness. She even opened her own nursing school, which is basically like a Hogwarts for nurses (except with less magic and more bedpans).

The OG Wonder Woman
Florence Nightingale inspired girls everywhere to become nurses and showed the world that girls can be strong leaders too. She's like the real-life Wonder Woman, but with a lamp instead of a lasso!

Florence Nightingale's Superpowers:
Leveled up nursing: Her ideas about cleanliness, training, and care transformed how nurses work and saved countless lives.
Slayed the germs: Florence's focus on hygiene stopped patients from getting sicker from dirty bandages – ew!

Empowered girls: She showed that girls can be heroes in the healthcare world too.

Florence Nightingale's bravery and dedication to helping others continue to inspire us today. So next time you see a nurse, remember Florence Nightingale, the battlefield babe who wasn't afraid to get her hands dirty and change the world, one bandage at a time!

Florence Nightingale: The Lady with the Lamp

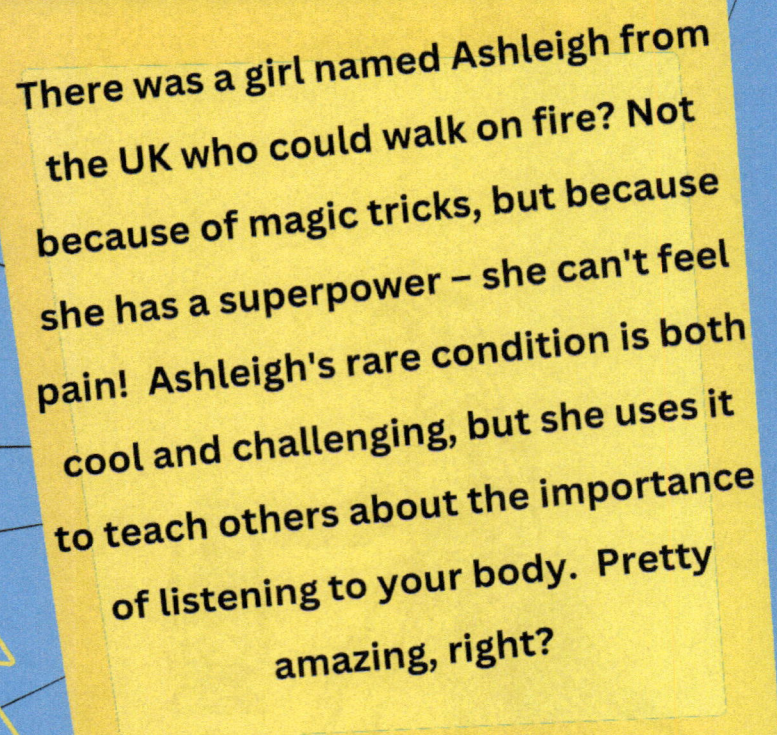

There was a girl named Ashleigh from the UK who could walk on fire? Not because of magic tricks, but because she has a superpower – she can't feel pain! Ashleigh's rare condition is both cool and challenging, but she uses it to teach others about the importance of listening to your body. Pretty amazing, right?

DID YOU KNOW?

Banting & Best, the Diabetic Dudes!

Imagine a world where getting a lunchtime sugar rush was a total nightmare, because your body couldn't handle it. That's what life was like for diabetics back in the day. But then two awesome scientists, **Frederick Banting & Charles Best**, swooped in like superheroes to battle the Sugar Monster!

Banting: The Relentless Doc

Born in 1891 (way before video games!), Frederick Banting wasn't your average doctor. He saw kids getting super sick from a condition called diabetes, and it totally bummed him out. He knew he had to find a way to help!

Best: The Brainy Buddy
Charles Best, born in 1899 (also way before

smartphones!), was a super smart student who wanted to be a doctor too. When he met Banting, it was like finding the ultimate science partner!

Summer of Science Smackdown!

In 1921, Banting and Best were like "summer vacation? Nah!" Instead, they holed up at a lab, working around the clock like they were trying to beat a video game on expert mode. Their mission: to find something in the body that could fight the Sugar Monster in diabetics. They experimented on dogs (with care, of course!), and finally discovered a secret weapon – a substance called **insulin**!!!!

From Lab to Life Saver!

This insulin stuff was like magic (but science-y magic!). When they injected it into diabetic dogs, their blood sugar levels went back to normal! This was a total game-changer. After more tests, they realized insulin could be a lifesaver for people with diabetes too.

Sharing the Victory!

In 1923, Banting and Best, along with another scientist who helped out, won a Nobel Prize, which is like a super science award! There were some high fives and maybe a little friendly arguing about who deserved more credit, but in the end, they were both heroes.

Banting and Best: A Legacy of Hope

Finding insulin didn't cure diabetes completely, but it was a super win! Diabetics could finally manage their condition and live normal lives. Banting and Best's work opened the door for even more scientific discoveries to help people with diabetes.

More Than Just Lab Rats!

The story of Banting and Best isn't just about cool science experiments. It shows how teamwork is super important, and that you shouldn't give up, even if finding a cure feels like the hardest video game level ever. Their dedication to helping others inspires scientists today to keep battling diseases.

Banting and Best's Superpowers:

Defeated the Sugar Monster: Their discovery of insulin gave diabetics a fighting chance against their condition.

Leveled Up Diabetes Treatment: They opened the way for even more research to help people with diabetes manage their health.

Teamwork Makes the Dream Work: Banting and Best showed that science is all about working together to achieve big goals.

Frederick Banting and Charles Best are true diabetic dudes! Their teamwork, perseverance, and scientific triumph continue to offer hope to people with diabetes all over the world. So next time you hear about insulin, remember these two scientists who faced the Sugar Monster head-on and saved the day!

The OG Doc Rock Star: Avicenna, the Prince of Physicians!

Imagine a world before hospitals and video game doctor simulators. That's the time **Ibn Sina**, also known as **Avicenna**, lived in, way back in 980 AD (that's like way before even sliced bread!). But even without fancy tools, Avicenna became a mega-doctor superstar!

A Bookworm Turns into a Medical Mastermind

Born in the city of Afshona , near Bukhara in Persia (think modern-day Iran and surrounding countries like Uzbekistan!), Avicenna wasn't just interested in video games (which they didn't have back then). He devoured books on everything – math, stars, even how the mind works. By 18, he knew SO much stuff, he was already a respected doctor!

Healing Like a Boss

Avicenna wasn't your average doc. He studied what ancient Greek doctors like **Hippocrates** knew, then added his own super-observations and experiments. He even wrote a giant medical book called "*The Canon of Medicine*" – basically a doctor's ultimate guidebook. This book was so awesome, it became required reading for doctors for centuries!

More Than Just Bandages: The Mind Matters Too!

Avicenna wasn't just about fixing broken bones. He also thought deeply about the brain and how it worked, like a real-life Dr. Phil of the past! He wrote about stuff like thinking, right and wrong, and even how our minds connect to the whole universe – pretty trippy, right?

A Legacy That Lives On

Avicenna's medical book and mind-bending ideas were translated into tons of languages, spreading his knowledge everywhere. He became a legend, and his work influenced doctors and thinkers for hundreds of years!

How Ibn Sina Rocked the World:

Leveled Up Medicine: His "Canon of Medicine" became the ultimate doc handbook, teaching doctors how to heal for centuries.

Mastered the Mind Game: His ideas about thinking, right and wrong, and the brain are still studied today – that's some serious brainpower!

Championed Observation: Avicenna believed in actually looking at stuff and experimenting, which is super important for science.

Avicenna's Legacy:

A medical pioneer: His work on healing the body laid the foundation for modern medicine.

A philosophical giant: His ideas about the mind continue to be studied and debated today.

A champion of critical thinking: Avicenna showed that asking questions and observing the world is key to understanding everything!

Ibn Sina, the OG doc rock star, reminds us that anyone can be a brainiac and change the world, even without fancy technology. So next time you visit the doctor, remember Avicenna, the medieval medic mastermind who started it all!

Ibn- Sina (Avicenna)
980 AD - 1037
Uzbekistan

DID YOU KNOW?

Your tongue is covered in tiny taste buds that help you enjoy all your favorite foods! There are five basic tastes: sweet, sour, salty, bitter, and umami (savory).

Stetho-Spy: René Laënnec's Heartbeat Heroics!

Imagine a doctor visit where the doc just poked you and guessed what was wrong. Yikes! That's how it was before **René Laënnec**, a super-smart French doctor, invented the stethoscope in 1816. This wasn't your grandpa's stethoscope though — it was like a spy gadget for listening to people's insides!

Bookworm Turns into a Mega-Doc

Born in France in 1781 (way before tablets!), René wasn't just glued to video games (they didn't have those yet). He loved science, especially how things worked. He became a doctor in Paris and was known for being super observant and totally dedicated to helping his patients.

The Birth of the Super-Hearer Gadget!

Here's where things get cool. René was treating a patient with a heart problem, but he couldn't hear her heartbeat clearly because, well, she was a little chubby. Not wanting to play guessing games, René rolled up some paper, like a makeshift spy microphone, and placed it on her chest. Boom! He could hear the heartbeat perfectly! This lightbulb moment led him to invent the stethoscope, a fancy tool with a tube that made listening to people's insides way easier. Doctors everywhere were like "Whoa, this Laënnec dude is a genius!"

From Listening to Lungs to Beating the Bad Guys

René wasn't just interested in hearts. He also studied lung diseases, especially this nasty one called tuberculosis. Thanks to his stethoscope and mad science skills, he figured out how this lung bully worked and how to fight it better. This was a major win for doctors everywhere!

Doc McStethoscope's Legacy

René Laënnec's stethoscope is like a doctor's ultimate gadget. It lets them hear all sorts of things inside people, helping them diagnose problems faster and more accurately. His work on lungs also helped countless people breathe easier. He wasn't just a mega-smart inventor, but also a super caring doctor who put his patients first.

How Laënnec Rocked the Medical World:

Leveled Up Doc Tools: His stethoscope gave doctors a superpower to hear what was going on inside people's bodies.

Became a Lung Legend: René figured out how lung diseases worked and how to fight them, making breathing easier for everyone.

Emphasized Patient Care: He wasn't just a gadget guy; René believed in listening to patients and treating them with care.

Laënnec's Legacy:

The OG of Listening: His work established listening to internal sounds as a key part of diagnosing diseases.

The Lung Whisperer: Laënnec's contributions are the foundation for modern lung medicine.

A Caring Doc Role Model: He showed that cool inventions and a caring bedside manner are a winning combo for doctors.

René Laënnec, the inventor of the stethoscope, reminds us that even a simple tool can change the world. So next time you see a doctor with a stethoscope, remember René Laënnec, the mega-doc who listened his way to saving countless lives!

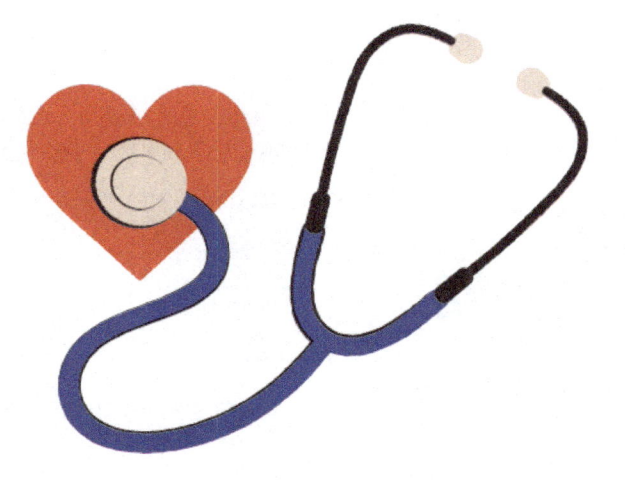

The Heart Hacker: Christiaan Barnard, the Doc Who Swapped Beating Boxes!

Imagine a world where a bad heart meant it was game over for real. That's what things were like before Dr. Christiaan Barnard, a super brave South African surgeon, performed the world's first human-to-human heart transplant in 1967. This wasn't your average surgery – it was like swapping out a broken video game controller for a brand new one... except way more intense!

IPPA photographer CC BY 4.0

From Cub Scout to Crazy (But Cool!) Surgeon

Born in 1922 (way before fancy surgery games!), Christiaan wasn't just into camping and tying knots. He was super curious about how the human body worked, especially the heart. This curiosity turned him into a doctor, and he wasn't afraid to try new things in the operating room, even if they seemed a little crazy at first.

A Totally Rad (But Scary) Idea: Stealing Hearts (For Good!)

Back then, if your heart went kaput, it was pretty much lights out. But Christiaan had a wild idea: what if you could take a healthy heart from someone who, sadly, couldn't use it anymore, and give it to someone whose heart was about to give up? It sounded impossible, but Christiaan wouldn't give up on his crazy dream. He spent years practicing this super tricky surgery and facing tons of doubt from other doctors who thought he was nuts.

The Big Operation: A Race Against the Clock!!

In 1967, the chance finally came. A young woman named Denise had a heart that was about to quit, and there was a car accident victim, Denise Darvall, who might be a match. With his A-team of super skilled nurses and assistants, Christiaan went into surgery mode. For 9 long hours, they carefully took out Denise's bad heart and put in the healthy one from the donor. The whole world held its breath!

A Short-Lived Miracle

The surgery was a success! The guy who got the new heart, Louis Washkansky, became the first person EVER to live with someone else's heart. It was like something out of a sci-fi movie! Sadly, back then, medicine to stop the body from rejecting the new heart wasn't perfect, and Louis's body eventually said "no thanks" to the new one. He passed away 18 days later.

A Legacy That Keeps on Tickin

Even though Louis didn't live forever, Christiaan Barnard's surgery was a total game-changer. It proved that swapping hearts was possible, and now doctors could save tons of people who would have otherwise died. His bravery and crazy ideas inspired a whole new era of organ transplant surgeries!

Dr. Barnard's Superpowers:

Pioneered Heart Swaps: He showed the world that heart transplants could actually work!

Leveled Up Transplant Medicine: His work led to better medicine to stop bodies from rejecting new organs.

Inspired Bold Doctors: He showed that taking risks in medicine can lead to amazing breakthroughs.

Christiaan Barnard's Legacy:

A Heart Transplant Hero: He paved the way for modern heart transplant surgery.

A Champion of Crazy Ideas: Barnard showed that even the wildest ideas can change medicine for the better.

A Symbol of Hope: His work continues to offer hope to people with heart problems and other life-threatening conditions.

Dr. Christiaan Barnard wasn't afraid to think outside the box. His groundbreaking surgery may not have saved Louis Washkansky permanently, but it opened the door for countless others to receive life-saving heart transplants. His story reminds us that sometimes, the coolest things in medicine come from people who dare to dream big and try something totally new!

❌ MYTHS

YOU SHOULD POP YOUR PIMPLES

✅ FACTS

Popping pimples can actually worsen them and lead to scarring. Your skin has its own way of healing blemishes, and picking at them can introduce bacteria and inflammation

The Smell Superstar: Dr. Linda B. Buck, the Queen of Funky Funky Smells!

Imagine a world where smells were just confusing blasts of weirdness, like a code no one could crack. That's what things were like before ***Dr. Linda B. Buck***, an awesome American scientist, discovered the secret code of smells in the 1990s. Her work basically showed us how our noses turn funky smells into awesome messages!

From Regular Kid to Super Sniffer Scientist

Born in 1947 (way before fancy smell-o-vision games!), Linda wasn't your typical kid. Sure, she liked playing outside, but she also had a super curious mind that loved figuring out how stuff worked. This curiosity led her to become a scientist who studied the amazing world of smells – way cooler than studying, like, rocks!

Cracking the Code of Funky Funky Smells

Scientists knew smells were important, but how our noses figured out all those different stinky, yummy, or just plain weird smells was a total mystery. Linda decided to tackle this super smelly riddle. She teamed up with another scientist, Richard Axel, and together they became the ultimate smell detectives!

Sniffing Their Way to a Super Science Award!!!

After years of sniffing out clues (not literally, hopefully!), Linda and Richard discovered a bunch of special genes in our noses that act like tiny keys. These keys fit into special locks shaped like different smells, letting our brains know exactly what funky odor we're smelling. Their discovery was a game-changer, and they even won a super prestigious science award, the Nobel Prize, in 2004, for figuring out the whole smell thing!

The Power of a Smelly Discovery!

Dr. Buck's work wasn't just about figuring out why pizza smells so good (although that's pretty important too!). Understanding smell can help us make new medicines, create way cooler artificial smells, and even understand some diseases better. Pretty awesome, right?

Dr. Buck's Superpowers:

Cracked the Smell Code: She discovered how our noses figure out all those different funky smells.

Opened Doors for New Stuff: Her work can help with medicine, smells, and even fighting diseases!

Inspired Future Scientists: Dr. Buck showed us that asking questions and exploring the unknown can lead to super cool discoveries.

Dr. Linda B. Buck's Legacy:

The Queen of Smelly Science: Her work is the foundation for everything we know about smell today.

A Champion of Asking Why: Dr. Buck's research shows that curiosity can lead to unexpected breakthroughs.

A Role Model for Girls in Science: Her Nobel Prize win is an inspiration for girls who want to be scientists too!

Dr. Linda B. Buck's work revolutionized the way we understand smell. Her discoveries remind us that even the weirdest stuff, like a gym sock or a blooming flower, holds hidden secrets waiting to be uncovered. So next time you take a big whiff of something funky, remember Dr. Linda B. Buck, the scientist who cracked the code of smell!

The OG Spare Parts Doc: Dr. Joseph Murray, the Kidney Kick-Starter!

Imagine a world where a busted kidney meant it was game over. That's what things were like before **Dr. Joseph Murray**, a super brave American surgeon, performed the world's first successful human kidney transplant way back in 1954. He wasn't just a doctor; he was a pit crew for failing organs, giving them a second chance to win the race of life!

From War Doc to Body Mechanic

Born in 1919 (way before cool surgery simulators!), Dr. Murray wasn't into boring stuff. Sure, he played games, but he was also super curious about the human body and how to fix it when it broke. This curiosity turned him into a surgeon. During World War II, he treated injured soldiers and saw firsthand how awful organ failure was. That's when he got a crazy (but awesome!) idea: what if you could take a healthy spare kidney from someone and give it to a person whose own kidney was failing?

Twin Power: The First Kidney Heist (But in a Good Way!)

Back then, transplanting organs seemed like something out of a superhero movie. But Dr. Murray had a plan. The key was using twins, since their bodies were like super compatible. In 1954, the chance came along. Richard and Ronald Herrick, twin brothers, had a problem – one twin's kidney was failing. Dr. Murray, with his team of A-star nurses and helpers, went into super surgery mode. They took a healthy kidney from Ronald and put it into Richard. And guess what? It worked! Richard's body accepted the new kidney, and he lived a long and healthy life!

Opening the Door for More Spare Parts Surgeries

Dr. Murray's success with the Herrick twins wasn't just a one-time thing. It was a game-changer! It showed that transplanting organs could actually save lives, and it inspired other doctors to try this surgery with different organs too. Dr. Murray's work was so amazing, he even shared a Nobel Prize in 1990!

Dr. Murray's Superpowers:

Started the Organ Transplant Party: His kidney transplant was the first successful one ever, paving the way for tons of other surgeries.

Used Super Compatible Twins: Dr. Murray figured out that twins were the best match for early transplants.

Inspired a Bunch of Doc Rookies: He showed other doctors that organ transplants could be a reality.

Dr. Joseph Murray's Legacy:

The Godfather of Transplants: He's considered the most important dude in the history of organ transplants.

A Champion of Trying New Stuff: Dr. Murray wasn't afraid to take risks, and his bravery changed medicine forever.

A Symbol of Hope: His work continues to offer hope to people with failing organs, giving them a second shot at life.

Dr. Joseph Murray wasn't afraid to think outside the box. His groundbreaking surgery on the Herrick twins might seem like a long time ago, but it totally transformed medicine. His story reminds us that even the weirdest ideas can lead to amazing breakthroughs, giving people second chances when they need them most. So next time you hear about an organ transplant, remember Dr. Joseph Murray, the OG spare parts doc, the guy who kick-started the whole organ transplant party!

DID YOU KNOW?

The human nose can distinguish over 1 trillion different scents! That's way more than your average perfume counter.

Dr. Crumpler: First Black Woman Doctor (Seriously!!!)

Imagine this, dude. Back in the 1800s, being a doctor was like, totally for guys with those creepy mustaches and top hats – even inside! Gross. But there was this awesome chick named **Rebecca Lee Crumpler** who wasn't having any of that. She became the very first Black woman doctor in the whole entire USA. Talk about breaking the mold!

She wasn't always a doctor, though. For like, eight whole years, she was a nurse, taking care of sick people. Like a school nurse, but way more intense. Probably way less dodgeball involved, though. Anyway, Rebecca saw a problem. Tons of women and kids, especially Black folks, couldn't get decent medical care. Some doctors wouldn't even see them! That's messed up, right? So Rebecca decided to become a doctor herself and fight for those who needed it most.

The only problem? Medical schools were basically like boys' clubs back then. They wouldn't let girls, especially Black girls, learn all that fancy doctor stuff. But Rebecca wasn't one to back down. She studied like crazy and finally convinced a special school in Boston to let her in. Can you imagine being the only girl in a class full of mustached dudes? Awkward City, population: YOU.

Guess what? In 1864, Rebecca graduated – Dr. Crumpler, the first Black woman doctor in the US! That's like being the first kid to ever dunk a basketball – history-making stuff! She opened her own practice in Boston, mostly treating women and kids. She even wrote a whole medical book called "*A Book of Medical Discourses*" to help moms take care of their little ones. Pretty impressive for someone who wasn't even supposed to be a doctor in the first place!

Dr. Crumpler's journey wasn't exactly a walk in the park. People sometimes made fun of her for being a doctor, but she never stopped helping people. She's a true legend, showing us that anyone can achieve their dreams, no matter what. So next time you see a doctor or hear about a cool science discovery, remember Dr. Rebecca Lee Crumpler, the trailblazing Black doctor who rocked the system and paved the way for others!

CROSSWORD

Across
2. Gives you medicine when you're sick
5. Bandaid is another word for this
8. First used to prevent smallpox
9. Wash your hands with this to kill germs
11. a tool helps doctors see tiny organs and tissues inside the body. (8 letters)
13. Studies diseases to find cures
14. AID Helps you hear better
15. Checks your temperature to see if you have a fever

Down
1. Bandages wrap around this
3. Stops bleeding
4. White blood cells fight these
6. Charted the first map of the human body
7. Stops you from getting sick.
8. (This is a trick question - answer written backward)
10. X-rays help doctors see your bones
12. Donates blood to help others

The Dude Who Saved Lives with... Stinky Spray?

Imagine this, dude. Back in the day, like the 1800s, surgery was a total nightmare. It was April 5th, 1827, and if you needed an operation, forget fancy painkillers! And guess what? Half the time you'd catch some gross infection and… well, let's just say things weren't pretty. That's where **Joseph Lister** comes in, the superhero who saved lives with... wait for it... stinky spray!

Lister wasn't just some random dude, though. He was born in Upton, England on April 5th, 1827, and his dad was a brainiac scientist, kind of like a real-life Willy Wonka, but without the chocolate factory (and hopefully less creepy). Young Joseph grew up curious about everything, and that curiosity led him to become a surgeon himself. But here's the thing: after surgery, most patients got infected and died! It was a total bummer.

Then came the weird part. Another scientist named Louis

Pasteur, like a germ detective, figured out that tiny invisible things called germs caused these infections. Lister was like, "Whoa, that explains a LOT!" But how to kill those sneaky germs? Here's the crazy part: Lister thought carbolic acid, which smelled like a gym sock factory exploded next to a rotten egg farm, could be the answer. Imagine the worst smell ever – that was carbolic acid!

Lister started spraying everything in the operating room with this stinky stuff – tools, bandages, even the air! People thought he was totally nuts, but guess what? It worked! Way fewer patients got infected. Lister became like the rockstar of surgeons, proving that stopping germs before surgery was the key.

Sure, the carbolic acid spray wasn't exactly a breath of fresh air, but it paved the way for how hospitals are clean and disinfected today. So next time you're at the doctor's and everything smells clean, thank Joseph Lister, the superhero who fought germs with a super-stinky spray!

The Body Dude: Andreas Vesalius and the Exploding Skeleton

Imagine dissecting a dead body in science class, but instead of a smelly frog, it's a whole human! That was totally normal back in the 1500s, and Andreas Vesalius, born on December 31st, 1514, in Brussels, Belgium (that's like France's cooler neighbor), was like the rockstar of dissecting dudes (and chicks, but mostly dudes).

Vesalius wasn't just some squeamish nerd, though. His family was big into medicine, and young Andreas travelled all over Europe, soaking up knowledge like a sponge. By the time he was 23, he was already a doctor – that's like becoming a brain surgeon before you can even legally drive!

The problem was, doctors back then relied on books written by this ancient Greek dude named Galen, who never actually dissected a human body himself. Crazy, right? So, Vesalius decided to ditch the dusty old books and become the ultimate body detective. He snuck into cemeteries (think creepy graveyard adventures at night!), bribed guards to get bodies from execution sites (eww!), and even convinced people to donate their dead relatives to science (which was a tough sell back then).

Dissecting dead bodies wasn't exactly a walk in the park. Imagine the smell! But Vesalius was determined. He discovered that Galen's books were full of mistakes — for example, Galen thought people had two jawbones, but Vesalius proved it was just one! Boom! Roasted ancient Greeks!

Vesalius wasn't just about showing up old doctors, though. He wanted everyone to learn about the human body, so he wrote a giant textbook with awesome pictures of muscles, bones, and organs — like a super gory science textbook, but way cooler! This book, called "On the Fabric of the Human Body," was a total hit, and it changed the way doctors understood anatomy forever.

Sadly, Vesalius's adventures didn't end well. He messed with some powerful people (including the king!), and they weren't exactly happy about him digging up dead bodies. He ended up on a pilgrimage (think a super long walk to apologize), but his ship got wrecked, and he died on a tiny island in Greece in 1564. Bummer, right?
Even though his life ended on a bad note, Andreas Vesalius is a

total legend. He showed us that questioning the old ways and getting your hands dirty (literally!) can lead to amazing discoveries. So next time you look in the mirror and flex your muscles, thank Andreas Vesalius, the body dude who dared to dissect and rewrite the history of medicine!

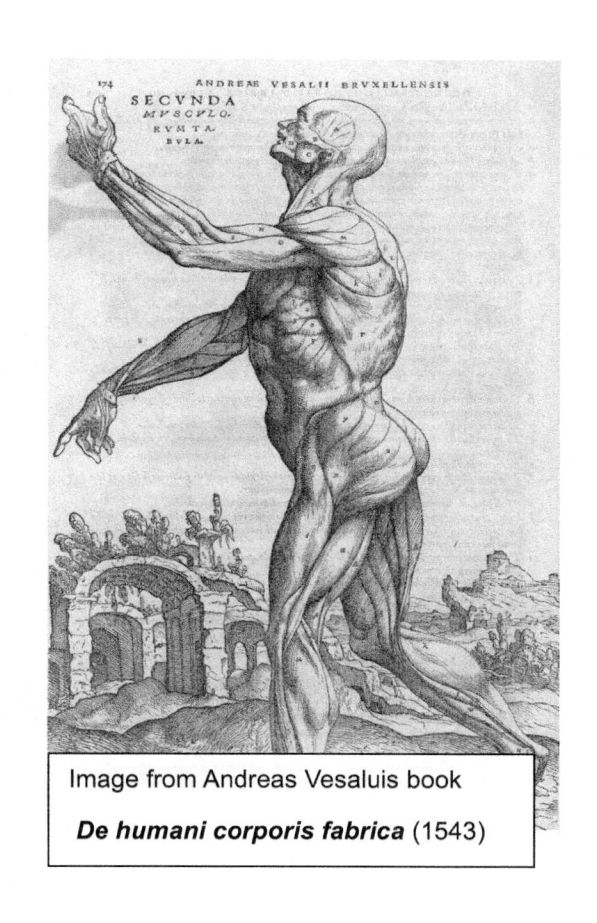

Image from Andreas Vesaluis book
De humani corporis fabrica (1543)

CROSSWORD SOLUTION

							¹w									
				²d	o	c	t	o	r							
							u									
					³g		n		⁴g							
				⁵b	a	n	d	a	g	e						
					u				r							
	⁶v				z				m		⁷v					
	e		⁸v	a	c	c	i	n	e		⁹s	o	a	p		
¹⁰b	s		a								c					
o	a		c				¹¹m	i	c	r	o	s	c	o	p	e
n	l		c		¹²d						i					
¹³e	p	i	d	e	m	i	o	l	o	g	i	s	t			
s	u		n		n						¹⁴h	e	a	r	i	n	g
s		¹⁵t	h	e	r	m	o	m	e	t	e	r			
					r											

Think about it
Would you Rather

- Would you rather have super strong muscles or super strong bones?
- Would you rather be able to taste everything or nothing at all?
- Would you rather have a hiccup that lasts for an hour or a sneeze that explodes your hair?

The End 🌟

"In the closing pages of our odyssey through the lives of extraordinary medical champions, we unveil narratives brimming with valor, compassion, and the enchantment of selflessness. These remarkable souls, akin to celestial bodies adorning the night sky, have etched indelible imprints upon the tapestry of history. Yet, amidst their luminous glow, lies a multitude of unsung heroes, each as remarkable as the next, who have contributed to the tapestry of medicine's evolution. Though they may have departed, their legacies endure, warming our spirits with an ineffable sense of gratitude. As you tenderly turn the final leaf and embark upon your own voyage, let their tales stir within you a profound sense of empathy and purpose. With every gesture of kindness, whether grand or modest, you assume the mantle of heroism, casting light upon a world often shrouded in shadows. Therefore, let your heart overflow with appreciation for these extraordinary souls, and may their enduring influence continue to guide us, even through the darkest of nights."

O! Check it out, dudes and dudettes
My name's Oussama, but everyone calls me Oss (easier to remember, right?). I'm from Algeria 🇩🇿,and guess what? I'm a real-life doctor ⚕️! Back in 2013, I graduated from Batna Medical Faculty (big words, I know). Being a doctor is awesome, but I wanted to do more to keep people healthy in the first place, not just fix them up after they get sick. So, I went back to school (ugh, more studying) and became a Medical Doctor Epidemiologist in 2021 (fancy title, huh?). Basically, I'm like a disease detective ♂, figuring out how to stop them before they even start!
Now, I'm the boss of the Prevention Department in Biskra (pretty cool, right). My job is all about making sure everyone stays healthy and happy .
This book? It's my way of sharing all the cool stuff I know about medicine with YOU!
Thanks for joining me on this wild ride through medical history. We met some pretty awesome scientists, right? Hopefully you learned a bunch of cool stuff and maybe even got a little inspired to be a future doctor yourself (or a disease detective like me, wink wink).😉👍
Remember, taking care of yourself and others is super important. Brush those teeth, eat your veggies (gross, I know, but trust me!), and wash your hands like a maniac (seriously, germs are everywhere!).
Speaking of the future, keep your eyes peeled for more books from yours truly. I've got a whole lot more fascinating stuff about medicine to share. Until then, stay healthy, stay curious, and remember – YOU have the power to make the world a healthier place!
Peace out!
Oss

ABOUT
me

Image Credits

Public Domain Images

The images included in this book are all in the public domain. These images have been selected to enhance the educational experience of this publication and are believed to be free of any copyright restrictions.

© 2024 Oussama Wail Bouhentala

All rights reserved.

This book is written by Oussama Wail Bouhentala

Contact the author: oussama.bouhentala@univ-biskra.dz

Printed in Great Britain
by Amazon